On the Track

by Claire Llewellyn   **illustrated by Mark Ruffle**

 CAMBRIDGE UNIVERSITY PRESS

 UCL Institute of Education

T0373840

What is athletics?

Athletics is the name for many different types of sport.

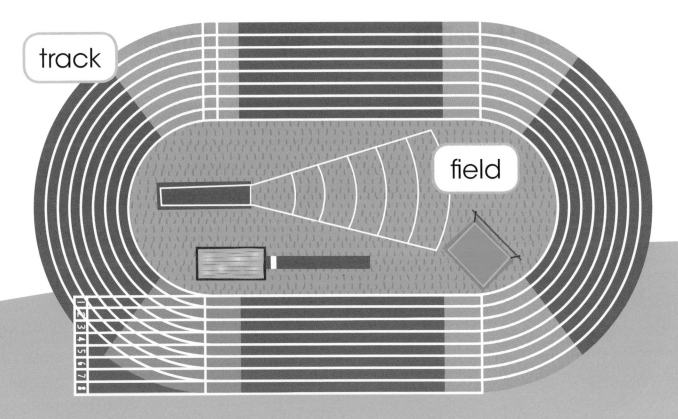

track

field

All the sports take place on a field or track.
People who run, jump and throw are called **athletes**.

sprinting

high jump

long jump

javelin

hurdles

Sprinting

finish line

running lane

1 2 3 4 5 6 7 8

starting block

The sprint is a short race.
The athletes have to run very fast.
The first one to finish is the **winner.**

How to sprint

1 Start to run when you hear 'Go!'

2 Use your arms and legs to run very fast.

3 Push your chest towards the finish line.

Hurdles

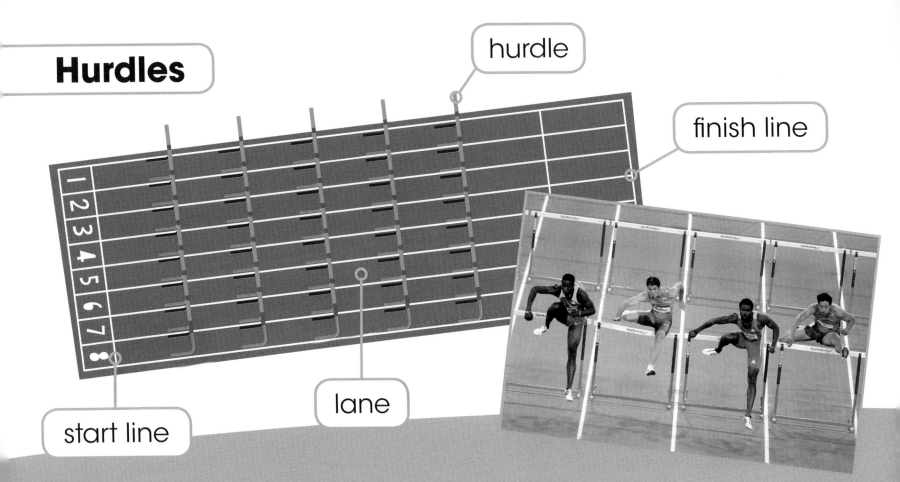

hurdle

finish line

lane

start line

Athletes run round the track
and jump over bars called **hurdles**.

They need to run fast and jump high.
The winner is the first one to cross the line.

How to jump over hurdles

1

GO!

Start to run when you hear 'Go!'

2

Lift your leg up and over the first hurdle.

3

Run as soon as you hit the track.

4

After the last hurdle, run fast towards the line.

The long jump

The long jump takes place on the field.

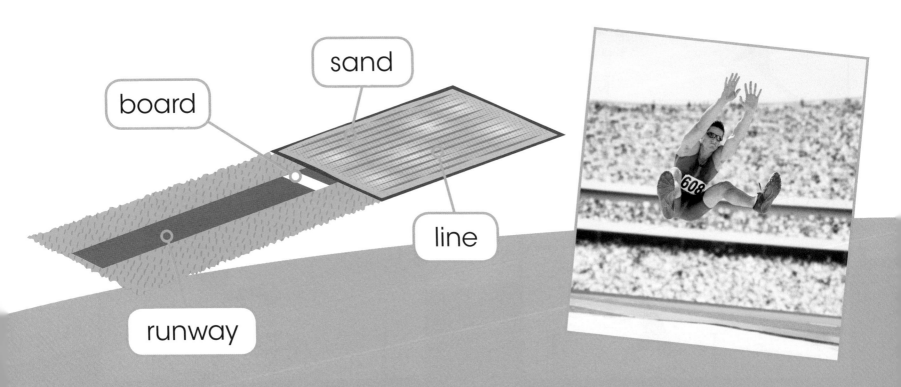

sand

board

line

runway

Athletes jump as far as they can into a pit of sand.

The winner is the athlete with the longest jump.

How to do the long jump

1 Run fast towards the board.

2 Hit the board and jump.

3 Land as far from the board as you can.

High jump

bar

soft mat

The high jump takes place on the field.
The athletes have to jump over a bar.
The bar is lifted higher and higher.
The winner is the person with the highest jump.

How to do the high jump

1

Run in a **curve** towards the bar.

2

Jump up high and turn in the air.

3

Arch your back, lift your hips and tip over the bar.

4

Land on the soft mat.

The javelin

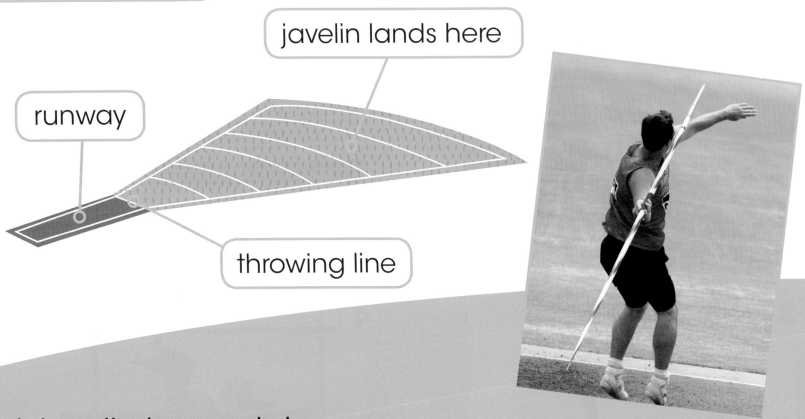

javelin lands here

runway

throwing line

A javelin is a metal **spear**.

Athletes throw the javelin as far as they can.

The winner is the person who throws it the furthest.

How to throw the javelin

1 Hold the javelin high and run towards the line.

2 Pull the javelin back as far as you can.

3 Lift your arm fast and let go of the javelin.

Glossary

athletes   people who are good at sport

curve   line that is not straight

hurdles   bars that athletes have to jump when running

spear   long, thin sharp metal or wood for throwing

winner   person that wins something

Index

On the Track ⬤ Claire Llewellyn

Reading notes written by Sue Bodman and Glen Franklin

Using this book

Developing reading comprehension

A non-fiction text of mixed genre, this book explores the various athletics track and field events. The non-chronological report element describes each sport, whilst procedural features are used in the 'How to ...' sports guides sections. Technical terms are defined in the glossary. Photographs and diagrams demonstrate the various processes involved in each sport.

Grammar and sentence structure

- Sentences follow the grammatical conventions for each genre, such as continuous present tense for report writing, and the use of imperative verbs when giving instructions.

- Labels are unpunctuated, demonstrating the correct convention for this non-fiction feature.

- Adverbial phrases ('towards the board', 'into a pit of sand') extend meaning in sentences.

Word meaning and spelling

- Unfamiliar, novel vocabulary is supported through the context and the glossary.

- Spelling of comparative and superlative adjectives ('high', 'higher', 'highest').

Curriculum links

PE – Children may not have experienced some of these athletic sports. Try some out during a PE lesson, ensuring the relevant safety measures are in place (and possibly omitting the javelin!).

History – Children may be studying ancient cultures such as the Greeks or Romans. Many of these athletic sports come from ancient times. For example, children could read about the origins of the Olympic Games in Greece in non-fiction texts and on the internet.

Learning Outcomes

Children can:

- solve novel, unfamiliar words using print information, checking to ensure the meaning is understood

- understand the different features of report and procedure (instructional) writing

- comment on what they have read, relating to their own experience.

A guided reading lesson

Book Introduction

Activate children's prior knowledge by discussing sports events they are familiar with, from schools sports days or from watching televised athletics events such as the Olympics. Read the title and the blurb with the children.

Orientation

Give a brief overview of the book, using sentence structures appropriate for both report and procedural texts: *In this book we find out about lots of different sports called athletics. The book even tells us how to we can do these sports.*

Preparation

Turn first to page 2 which provides an introduction to the book. Provide the children with the word 'athletics' locating it both in the heading and in the main text. Look at the word 'athletes', noting it is a glossary word, and ask the children to look up the definition.

Remind the children about the purpose of non-fiction texts, and that they are not usually read from cover to cover. Look at the chart on page 3, which lists the names of the different sports events featured in the book. Practise reading the names of the different sports, using phonic knowledge and looking for known chunks (such as /ing/). It might help to have the words on a white board or flip chart.